To the students and teachers
of Haddonfield Friends School.
-Tr. Stacey 2010

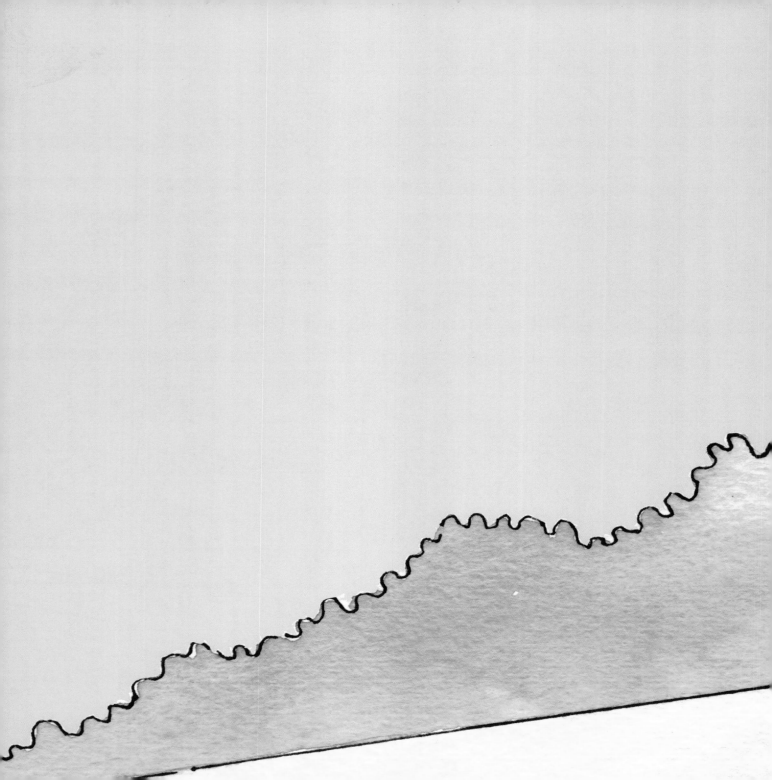

We're Going to Meeting!

Written and Illustrated by
Stacey Currie

We're going to Meeting for Worship today.

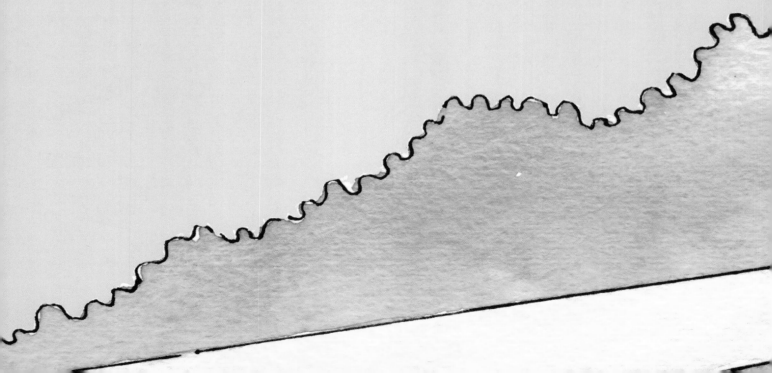

It's fun to run around or talk with our friends, but we can enjoy quiet times together, too.

When we go to Meeting for Worship, it's time to be peaceful and silent.

We line up quietly with our class.

We see our friends in the hallway and give them quiet waves.

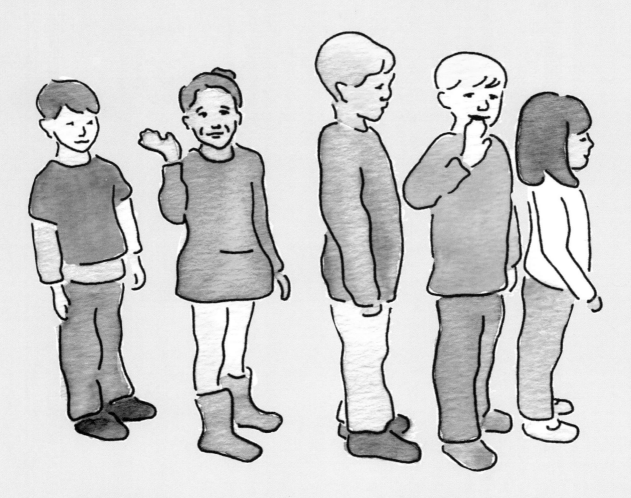

Our friends are going to Meeting, too!

We sit on a bench with our class and settle into silence. Lots of kids and teachers are sitting nearby. Our eyes might be closed, but don't worry, we're not sleeping!

When we keep our hands to ourselves and try not to wiggle much, we help the older kids and grown-ups settle into silence.

When we're all silent, we can think about the things we're thankful for, or the things we're worried about, or anything at all!

We can think about our fish.

We can think about our family and friends.

When someone we know is sick or hurt,
we can hold them in the Light.

We can think all our thoughts to God.

God listens when we think...
and we can listen to God.

Sometimes, kids have something special to say. We like to listen to them share with us. We might have something to say, too!

When Meeting is over,
we all shake hands and say,
"Good morning!"

We'll go to Meeting again soon, but now it's time to run, and shout, and play!

About Meeting for Worship

Meeting for Worship is the heart of the Friends school community. However, many students and teachers within Friends schools are not Quaker and at first, Meeting for Worship can be a bit of a mystery.

Meeting for Worhsip is a time to cooperatively seek the guidance of God knowing that "where two or three are gathered in my name, there am I in the midst of them" (Matthew 18:20). In many ways, Meeting for Worship is like a church service, but is unprogrammed, without any one person "in charge." Friends quiet their minds and voices while centering their thoughts to pray or wait expectantly for the still small voice of God or the "Inner Light." Worshiping in silence may initially feel unnatural for some, but is ultimately enjoyable and worthwhile for all.

Those attending enter the Meeting House in silence and quietly take their seats, careful not to disturb those already present. Being comfortable and free from the temptation to chat or wiggle can be helpful, so those accompanying children should chose seats wisely. Quiet meditation can begin immediately, or relaxation techniques may be used to quiet oneself. Silence may be broken by a member of the group who stands to share a message which he or she feels moved to speak. After someone shares, it is time to reflect inwardly on the insight provided. It is appropriate to wait several minutes before sharing an additional message. Sometimes, no one speaks at all, but in Meetings full of children, messages often abound! After about an hour, Friends close Meeting by shaking hands and greeting each other with smiles and words.

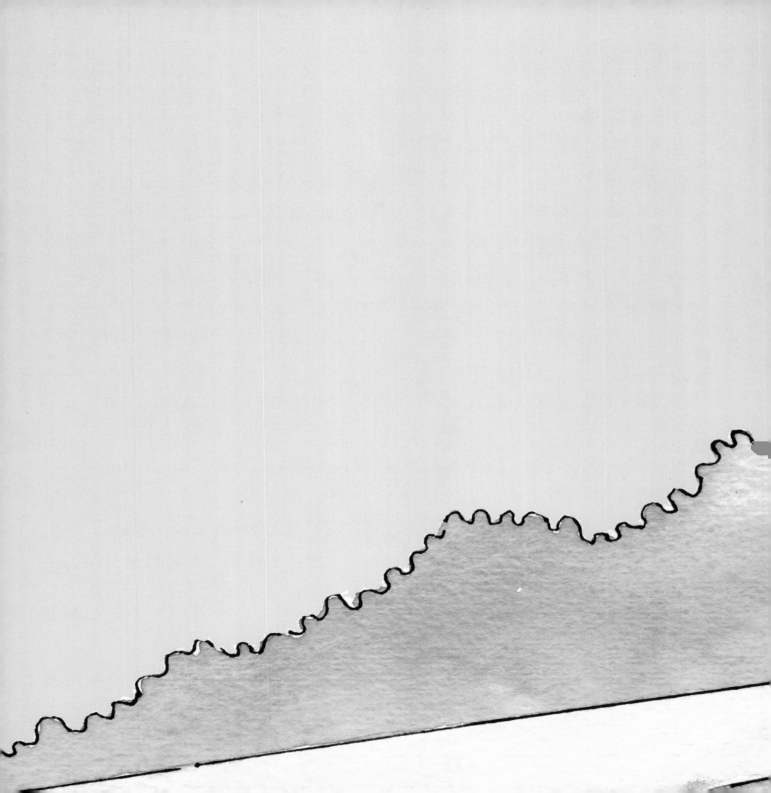